Everything That Matters in the Kitchen

kids CAN Cook

Cook Book

by Dianne Linderman

Illustrated by Delores Uselman Johnson

dianne@EverythingThatMattersRadio.com
Grants Pass, OR 97526

www.EverythingThatMattersInThe Kitchen.com

Copyright 2014
Kids Can Cook
Cook Book

All rights reserved. No part of this book may be reproduced or utilized in any form or by any means, electronic or mechanical, including photocopying and recording, or by any information storage and retrieval system, without permission in writing from the publisher.

ISBN 978-1500965938

Dianne Linderman has three things she loves in life (besides her family) .... kids, cooking and animals!

Dianne's famous, "Everything That Matters in the Kitchen" traveling cooking shows have been a kid magnet. Noticing that kids always occupy the front row seats at her shows, she created a new show called "Kids Can Cook" to inspire kids and also give them a chance to cook alongside her on the stage.

This cook book is full of simple, healthy recipes that kids can make when they come home from school. Instead of popping a processed snack or meal in the microwave, they can take a few ingredients and create a delicious, simple and healthy snack or meal.

The recipes in this cook book are easy enough even for adults! Have fun cooking simple, healthy and incredibly delicious recipes!

Dianne Linderman

Dedicated to my children, Luke & Alexandra,
my husband, David, my Mom & Dad,
my 4 brothers and their wives,
my 17 nieces and nephews and grand nephew.

Contents

Breads, Crackers, Pizza
and more...

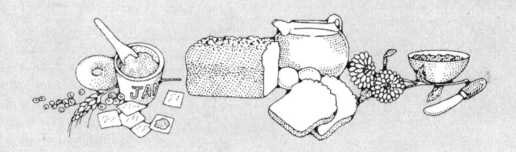

Farmhouse Crackers

This recipe makes 16 crackers. You may want to double up this batch!

- 1 cup **WHOLE WHEAT PASTRY FLOUR**
- 1 cup **OAT FLOUR**
- ½ teaspoon **BAKING POWDER**
- ½ teaspoon **SALT**
- 2 tablespoons chilled **BUTTER,** cut into small pieces
- 1/3 cup **WATER**
- 1 tablespoon **HEAVY CREAM**

Preheat oven to 300°.

Lightly spoon flours into dry measuring cups.

Pour flours, baking powder and salt into a large bowl and stir with a whisk.

Cut in butter with a pastry blender or knives until mixture looks like coarse meal.

Add 1/3 cup water and heavy cream; stir to form a stiff dough.

Roll dough into a 13-inch square on a baking sheet. Score dough into 16 equal squares. Pierce each cracker with a fork.

Bake for 45 minutes or until crisp. Cool on pan.

2

How to Make Butter

This is a fun thing to do!

Put as much Heavy Cream as you like in a jar with lid and shake (or use your blender) until solid (butter) separates from the liquid (whey).

Pour off whey through cheesecloth, then rinse off butter and add salt. Or, for my favorite, leave unsalted for sweet butter.

Healthy
Pizza Dough

- 1½ teaspoons **ACTIVE DRY YEAST**

- 1 1/4 cups **LUKEWARM WATER**

- 1 teaspoon **SUGAR** or **MAPLE SYRUP**

- 3 teaspoons **KOSHER SALT**

- 2 tablespoons **EXTRA-VIRGIN OLIVE OIL**

- 1 3/4 cups **WHOLE WHEAT PASTRY FLOUR**

- 1 3/4 cups **OAT FLOUR**

Preheat oven to 350°.

Place yeast in a bowl with ½ cup lukewarm water and one teaspoon of sugar or maple syrup. Let yeast bloom for a few minutes.

In a bowl, stir together 2½ cups of flour and the salt. Add the yeast mixture, oil and rest of the water. Mix with mixer or by hand very well. If you have a mixer with a dough hook, this would be the time to use it.

Turn mixer on and add remaining ingredients slowly. Dough should be pliable and elastic. This takes about 10 minutes.

Shape dough into 4 balls. Place the balls on a lightly floured plate, cover with plastic wrap and let rest for 15 minutes.

Roll dough on a floured pizza pan and poke a few holes in it with a fork. Bake for 5 to 10 minutes, or until desired crispiness is achieved.

Remove from oven and add yummy stuff! Bake for an additional 5-10 minutes.

Quick Whole Wheat
Pizza Dough

- 1 (.25 ounce) package **ACTIVE DRY YEAST**
- 1 cup **WARM WATER**
- 2 cups **WHOLE WHEAT FLOUR**
- 1/4 cup **WHEAT GERM**
- 1 teaspoon **SALT**
- 1 tablespoon **HONEY**

Preheat oven to 350°.

In a small bowl, dissolve yeast in warm water. Let stand until foamy, about 10 minutes.

In a large bowl, combine flour, wheat germ and salt. Make a well in the middle and add honey and yeast mixture. Stir well to combine. Cover and set in a warm place to rise for a few minutes.

Roll dough on a floured pizza pan and poke a few holes in it with a fork.

Bake for 5 to 10 minutes, or until desired crispiness is achieved.

Remove from oven and add yummy stuff! Bake for an additional 5-10 minutes.

Grilled Pizza

CRUST

- 1 teaspoon **MAPLE SYRUP**
- 2 packets **ACTIVE DRY YEAST**
- 2 teaspoons **OLIVE OIL**, plus extra for coating bowl
- **SALT** and **PEPPER**
- 2 ½ cups **WHOLE WHEAT PASTRY FLOUR**

TOPPINGS

I like use **NEWMAN'S TOMATO BASIL MARINARA SAUCE** and quality **MOZZARELLA CHEESE** and then top with fresh **TOMATO** and **BASIL** after grilling. You can add any type of **VEGGIES** or **COOKED MEATS**, or even make it a taco pizza. Be creative and have fun!

Combine syrup and yeast in a bowl with 1 cup of warm water and let stand until foamy. Add rest of crust ingredients and mix well.

Turn onto a floured board and knead until dough feels soft.

Place the dough inside a large bowl that has been coated with olive oil and let it stand until it doubles in size. Punch it down and knead it once more on a floured board. Place it back in the bowl and let rise again.

continued. . .

6

Heat the BBQ grill.

Place the dough back on the floured board and cut it into four sections.

With a floured rolling pin, roll out a section of dough into a round crust.

Brush one side of the dough with oil.

Lay the dough round on the BBQ grill, olive-oil-brushed-side down. Brush the top of the dough with a thin layer of olive oil, too. Let the dough cook for about 3 minutes, with the lid off.

Flip the dough over with tongs or spatula. Spread with a thin layer of sauce, then add cheese and top with your favorite ingredients—anything goes!

Close lid and let bake for approximately 3 to 5 minutes. Keep an eye on the pizza; you will know when it's done.

Eggs, Breakfast
and more...

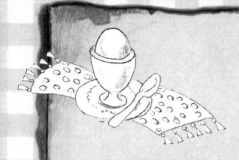

Dianne's Famous
Quiche

- ½ cup **HEAVY CREAM**
- 8 **EGGS**, beaten
- Any kind of **SAUTÉED VEGGIES** you would like to add—my favorites are spinach, mushroom, and tomato OR just basil and tomato.
- 3 to 4 cups your choice of grated **CHEESE**
- **SALT & PEPPER** to taste
- Prepared **WHOLE WHEAT PASTRY SHELL** (optional)

Preheat oven to 400°.

Bake pastry shell in a pie dish for 10 minutes. Or, for a low-carb recipe, don't use a pastry shell; just spray olive oil spray onto a glass pie dish.

Beat eggs, then stir in cream.

Place all veggies in baked pastry shell, then add cheese and salt & pepper.

Cover with scrambled egg mixture leaving room at the top for the quiche to puff up.

Bake for approximately 45 minutes to an hour. You can tell the quiche is done when it does not appear runny and does not jiggle.

Optional: Serve with a big green salad or use this as a breakfast entrée

Mini Egg Muffins

- 6 EGGS
- ½ cup **HEAVY CREAM**
- 1 cup **ONION**, chopped
- 3/4 cup Low-Fat **CHEESE** (Laughing Cow Cheese)
- **BROCCOLI,** or any other **VEGGIES** or none at all
- **SAUTÉED ONION**
- **SALT & PEPPER**
- **TOMATO**

This recipe is so easy! These mini quiche-type muffins are great for putting in your lunch or serving for breakfast, and you can add anything you like.

Preheat oven to 375°.

Spray each hole in a muffin pan with olive oil spray.

Scramble eggs.

Put veggies and cheese in each muffin tin first, now pour egg in and make sure you leave a little room for the mixture to puff up as it bakes. It is a little like a soufflé as it will puff up and then shrink after you take it out of the oven.

Bake for approximately 10 to 15 minutes. You can tell they are done by pressing your finger on them; they should feel firm.

Serve with some salsa. Yum!

11

Healthy
Pumpkin Pancakes

- 1 cup **WHOLE WHEAT FLOUR**
- 1 cup **OAT FLOUR**
- 2 tablespoons **COCONUT SUGAR** (or use a stevia baking blend)
- 2 ½ teaspoons **BAKING POWDER**
- ½ teaspoon **SALT**
- 1 teaspoon **CINNAMON**
- ½ teaspoon **ALLSPICE**
- ½ teaspoon **GINGER**
- 2 cups nonfat **MILK**
- 1 teaspoon **VANILLA**
- 3 tablespoons or more of **COCONUT OIL**
- 1 cup canned **PUMPKIN**

Mix all the dry ingredients together in a bowl.

Mix all the wet ingredients in with the dry ingredients until there are no clumps.

Cook on medium heat until the edges look dry, then flip. Remember, these pancakes will be dense and thick. This is how they are supposed to turn out.

Serve with **REAL MAPLE SYRUP!**

Ultimate
Breakfast Burrito

This is where you can get creative if you have left-over meat, chicken, fish or veggies. A low-carb tortilla makes a great breakfast, lunch, or dinner burrito.

- Large low carb or **WHOLE WHEAT TORTILLA** or **PITA BREAD**
- **SCRAMBLED EGGS**
- **SAUTÉED ONION**
- **SAUTÉED SPINACH** or other Veggies
- Any type of **MEAT, CHICKEN OR FISH**
- **SHREDDED CHEESE** of your choice
- **BLACK BEANS** (refried or whole)
- **VEGGIES**
- **SALSA**

Place tortilla on paper plate, add all of the ingredients, and fold like a burrito.

Put a wet paper towel on top of the burrito to keep it moist. Heat in oven at 300° or warm in microwave. Serve with salsa.

For a lunch or dinner burrito use any meat, chicken or fish. You can use left-overs or a store-bought rotisserie chicken. Then add all the goodies of your choice...black beans, cilantro, tomatoes, cheese, veggies, salsa... be creative!

Soups

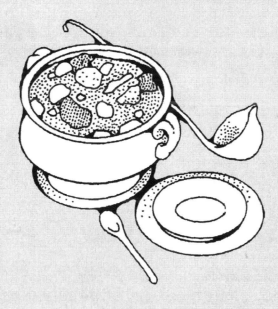

Creamy Cauliflower Soup

- 2 **CAULIFLOWER HEADS,** chopped
- 1 **MAUI SWEET ONION,** chopped
- 2 stalks **CELERY,** chopped
- 1 cup **PARSLEY,** minced
- 4 to 6 cups **CHICKEN BROTH,** or enough to cover cauliflower
- 2 **GARLIC CLOVES,** minced
- 1 cup **HEAVY CREAM**
- 1 cup shredded **CHEDDAR CHEESE**
- **SALT & PEPPER** to taste

In a large pot over medium heat, simmer cauliflower, onion, garlic, celery and parsley in chicken broth until soft.

Blend in a blender being careful not to put too much hot soup in the blender. You can blend half of the soup if you like chunky soup.

Add the cream, cheese, salt, and pepper to taste.

Don't over heat the soup once cream and cheese are added.

This is a delicious soup and will stick to your ribs. It is very low in carbs.

Creole Jambalaya

- 2 tablespoons **BUTTER** or **COCONUT OIL**
- 1 large **SWEET ONION**, chopped
- 8 **GREEN ONIONS**, chopped
- 2 **CELERY RIBS**, chopped
- 3 cups (1 lb.) **COOKED HAM**, cubed (organic or non-nitrate ham)
- 1 pound **CAJUN** or **SMOKED SAUSAGE**, sliced
- 1 8-oz can **TOMATO SAUCE**
- **GARLIC SALT** to taste
- **PEPPER** to taste
- 1/4 ground **RED PEPPER**
- 2 cups **TINY SHRIMP**
- 5 cups **BROWN RICE**, uncooked

Melt butter in a large skillet.

Add onions and celery; sauté until tender.

Add ham, sausage and the next 4 ingredients. Cook for 20 minutes while stirring.

Stir in rice. Cover and cook, stirring occasionally, on low heat for 30 minutes.

Before serving, add shrimp and stir in.

Serves 4 to 8 hungry men!

17

Gumbo

- 4 to 6 pieces of **CHICKEN**, dark or light
- **GARLIC SALT & PEPPER**, to taste
- 1/4 cup **OLIVE OIL**
- 1 pound Nitrate-free, **SMOKED SAUSAGE**, cut into 1/4-inch slices
- ½ cup **OAT FLOUR**
- 5 tablespoons **BUTTER**
- 1 large **SWEET ONION**, chopped
- 8 cloves **GARLIC**, minced
- 1 **GREEN BELL PEPPER**, seeded and chopped
- 3 stalks **CELERY**, chopped
- 1/4 cup **WORCESTERSHIRE SAUCE**

- 1/4 bunch **FLAT LEAF PARSLEY**, stems & leaves coarsely chopped, chopped leaves for garnish
- 4 cups **BEEF BROTH**
- 1 (14-ounce can) **STEWED TOMATOES** with juice
- 2 cups frozen **SLICED OKRA**
- 4 **GREEN ONIONS**, white and green parts sliced
- ½ pound small **SHRIMP**, peeled, deveined and cooked
- 6 cups **BROWN RICE** cooked in Chicken Broth

continued...

Season the chicken with garlic salt and pepper.

Heat the oil in a heavy bottomed Dutch oven over medium-high heat. Cook the chicken until browned on both sides and remove.

Add the sausage and cook until browned, then remove.

Make a roux: Sprinkle the flour over the oil. Add 2 tablespoons of butter and cook over medium heat, stirring constantly, until brown—about 10 minutes. Let it cool.

Return the Dutch oven to low heat and melt the remaining 3 tablespoons of butter. Add the onion, garlic, green pepper and celery and cook for 10 minutes.

Add Worcestershire sauce, salt and pepper to taste, and the 1/4 bunch parsley. Cook, while stirring frequently, for 10 minutes.

Add 4 cups hot beef broth, whisking constantly.

Add the chicken and sausage. Bring to a boil, then reduce the heat, cover, and simmer for 45 minutes.

Add tomatoes and okra. Cover and simmer for 1 hour.

Just before serving add the green onions, shrimp and chopped parsley.

Serve over brown rice.

Real Jewish
Chicken Noodle Soup

- 1 large whole **CHICKEN**, rinsed

- 3 large **CARROTS**, chopped

- 3 stalks **CELERY**, chopped into large pieces

- 1 **MAUI SWEET ONION**, chopped

- 1 whole bunch **PARSLEY**, finely chopped

- 2 cloves **GARLIC**, minced (optional)

- **SALT & PEPPER** to taste

- 2 cups **NOODLES**, pre-cooked, or **RICE** (brown rice is delicious!)

In a large soup pot, combine all the ingredients except the noodles or rice.

Add enough water to cover ingredients. Place a lid on the pot and simmer over medium heat for approximately 1 hour and 15 minutes.

Cook noodles or rice.

Allow soup to cool slightly. Skim soup of all visible fat, return to stove and warm on medium heat.

To serve:
Place noodles or rice and chicken pieces into individual bowls. Ladle hot soup over it and serve immediately.

This soup is great when you get a cold!

Salmon Chowder

- 2 tablespoons **BUTTER**
- ½ cup **ONION,** chopped
- 4 cloves **GARLIC,** minced
- 2 stalks **CELERY,** chopped
- 3 unpeeled **RED POTATOES,** chopped
- 4 tablespoons fresh **PARSLEY,** minced
- 7 ounces cooked **SALMON,** de-boned
- **GARLIC SALT & PEPPER** to taste
- 1½ cups **HEAVY CREAM** (optional)
- 4 to 6 cups **CHICKEN BROTH** or Clam Juice
- 2 tablespoons fresh or **DRIED DILL,** chopped
- 1/4 cup **WHITE WINE**
- 2 tablespoons **HONEY** or **MAPLE SYRUP**

Melt butter in a frying pan over medium heat. Add chopped onions, garlic, and celery and sauté them until translucent.

In large soup pot, place all ingredients except cream and honey. Add enough broth to just cover ingredients. Simmer until potatoes fall apart.

Using a hand or regular blender, purée ½ of the soup. Remove from heat and add cream. Taste the soup to see if adding a little honey could bring out the flavor.

Simple
Mushroom Soup

- 1 **LEEK**
- 2 to 3 pounds **MUSHROOMS** of choice, washed and sliced
- 1 tablespoon **BUTTER**
- 4 cups **CHICKEN BROTH**
- 2 tablespoons **OAT FLOUR**
- ½ cup dry **WHITE WINE**
- 3 tablespoons **FLAT LEAF PARSLEY,** minced
- **BLACK PEPPER**
- 2/3 cup **HEAVY CREAM**

Cut leek in half and finely chop white and green parts.

Place butter in a small saucepan and sauté leek and mushrooms over medium heat.

In a soup pot, add the rest of the ingredients, except the cream, and bring to a boil. Turn heat to low, and simmer for 15 minutes.

Blend half of the soup safely in a blender, add it to the remaining soup in the pot, and then stir in the cream.

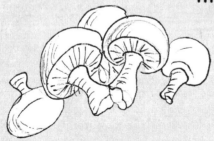

22

Split Pea Soup

- 1 pound dry **SPLIT PEAS**
- 1 **HAM BONE**
- 4 cloves **GARLIC**, minced
- 2 tablespoons each **BUTTER** and **OLIVE OIL**
- ½ pound **BABY CARROTS**, chopped
- 1 whole **SWEET ONION**, minced
- **GARLIC SALT & PEPPER** to taste

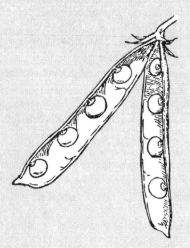

Empty package of split peas into a colander or bowl, and sort through well, removing foreign matter and imperfect peas. Rinse well.

Put peas into large soup pot along with ham bone and add enough water to cover peas.

In a frying pan, sauté the garlic, carrots and onion in butter and olive oil over medium heat. Add to soaking peas (add water if needed to just cover ingredients).

Add garlic salt and pepper to taste. Simmer on low for about an hour, stirring occasionally— or bake in oven at 375° for 2 hours. (Baking in the oven keeps it from burning.)

Tomato Basil Soup

- 6 to 8 large vine-ripened, organic **TOMATOES**

- 1 cup fresh **BASIL**

- 1 cup **WHOLE CREAM** or **WHOLE MILK** (optional)

- 2 cups **CHICKEN BROTH**

- 3 to 4 cloves fresh **GARLIC**, diced

- **GARLIC SALT & PEPPER** to taste

- 1/8 cup **WHITE WINE** (optional)

- 1 to 3 tablespoons **MAPLE SYRUP**, unless tomatoes are really sweet

- **TABASCO** or other hot sauce (if you like spicy soup)

- **FRESH BASIL** (optional, for garnish)

Purée all ingredients in a blender. If you want chunky soup, blend half of the soup a little less.

Warm, don't cook this soup for optimum health.

Don't be afraid to experiment and add ingredients like Parmesan cheese.

Garnish with some fresh basil.

Salads & Salad Dressings

Corn Salad

- 6 ears raw **CORN**, husked, cleaned
- 3 large **TOMATOES**, diced
- 1 large **ONION**, diced
- 1/4 cup fresh **BASIL**, chopped
- 1/4 cup **OLIVE OIL** or **GRAPE SEED OIL**
- 2 tablespoons **WHITE BALSAMIC VINEGAR**
- **SALT** and **PEPPER** to taste

Bring a large pot of lightly salted water to a boil.

Cook corn in boiling water for 7 to 10 minutes, or until desired tenderness.

Drain, cool, and cut kernels off the cob with a sharp knife.

In a large bowl, toss together the corn, tomatoes, onion, basil, oil, vinegar, salt and pepper.

Chill until serving.

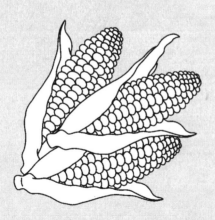

Cucumber Salad
with Tomato & Sweet Onion

- 4 **CUCUMBERS**, any type
- 2 **TOMATOES**, medium, sweet, vine ripened
- ½ **SWEET ONION**, large

Dressing
- 3 to 4 tablespoons (more or less) **WHITE BALSAMIC VINEGAR**
- 3 tablespoons **OLIVE OIL**
- **GARLIC SALT & PEPPER** to taste

Peel cucumbers if necessary, and slice. (I have been using lemon cucumbers—yum!).

Slice or cut tomatoes into small wedges.

Slice and cut onions.

For the dressing, whisk all ingredients together well. For best results, place dressing in the refrigerator for a few hours before serving, stirring occasionally.

Combine in a serving bowl and gently pour dressing, mixing well.

Strawberry & Spinach Salad with Chicken

- 2 bunches **BABY SPINACH**, rinsed

- 4 cups sliced **STRAWBERRIES**

- ½ cup **OLIVE OIL**

- 1/4 cup **BALSAMIC VINEGAR**

- 1/4 cup **MAPLE SYRUP**

- 1/4 teaspoon **PAPRIKA**

- 2 tablespoons **SESAME SEEDS**

- 1 tablespoon **POPPY SEEDS**

- 2 cups **CHICKEN**, cooked and shredded

In a large bowl, toss together the spinach and strawberries.

In a medium bowl, whisk together the oil, vinegar, syrup, paprika, sesame seeds, and poppy seeds.

Pour over the spinach and strawberries, and toss to coat.

You can also add chicken or shrimp.

Layered Berry & Melon Salad

In a beautiful glass bowl, layer Watermelon, Honeydew Melon, Cantaloupe, Raspberries, Strawberries, Blueberries, Grapes, etc.

Squeeze a little Lime Juice and drizzle a little Pure Maple Syrup on the berries. Keep layering until you get to the top.

Best Ever
Potato Salad

- 4 pounds **RED POTATOES**, washed
- 1 whole **MAUI SWEET ONION**, chopped
- 1 whole **PARSLEY** bunch, chopped
- 1 to 2 cups **VEGENAISE** (egg-free mayonnaise)
- 4 stalks **CELERY**, chopped
- 4 tablespoons **MUSTARD**
- 2 tablespoons **CELERY SALT**
- 3 tablespoons **SALAD SUPREME SEASONING** (any brand)
- 2 tablespoons **DRIED BASIL**
- **GARLIC SALT & PEPPER**, to taste

Boil potatoes until soft, but not mushy. Remove from heat and drain. Let stand for 15 minutes. You will notice that some of the skins has begun to peel away. Peel the skins that comes off easily, and leave the rest on. Cool potatoes to room temperature.

Cut potatoes into cubes, place in a large bowl with all other ingredients, and mix well using your hands or a large spoon. Taste and add extra salt as needed.

Refrigerate for 2 hours and devour!

29

Creamy Lime Dressing

- 2 tablespoons fresh **CILANTRO**, chopped
- 1 tablespoon **RED WINE VINEGAR**
- 1 teaspoon **LIME ZEST**
- 1/4 cup **LIME JUICE**
- ½ cup **SOUR CREAM** (can use non-fat)
- 1 clove **GARLIC**, smashed
- 1 tablespoon **HONEY**
- ½ cup **EXTRA VIRGIN OLIVE OIL** or **FLAX OIL**
- **SALT & PEPPER** to taste

Blend Creamy Lime Dressing ingredients until smooth and refrigerate.

Drizzle dressing over salad and serve immediately.

Delicious
Lemon Salad Dressing

- 2 LEMONS (or more)

- 1/8 cup OLIVE OIL or GRAPE SEED OIL

- GARLIC SALT & PEPPER to taste

- PARMESAN CHEESE, optional

The only way to make this dressing perfect is to actually have your salad ready to toss.

On a completely ready salad, squeeze lemons and add rest of ingredients.

Taste your salad after you toss it and see if it needs more of any of the above ingredients. It always depends on the amount of salad you use—this recipe is for at least 6 cups of salad.

Flax Oil & Balsamic Salad Dressing

- ½ cup FLAX OIL

- Less than ½ cup of BALSAMIC VINEGAR

- GARLIC SALT to taste

- PARMESAN CHEESE (optional)

Whisk all ingredients well. Pour over salad, and toss.

Sandwiches

Avocado Sandwich

- 2 slices **WHOLE GRAIN BREAD**
- **MAYONNAISE** or **VEGENAISE**
- **LETTUCE** and/or **SPROUTS**
- **CUCUMBER**
- **PICKLE**
- **TOMATO**
- **AVOCADO**
- **LEMON**
- **SALT & PEPPER**
- **CHEESE,** of your choice

Spread mayo on one slice of bread and layer veggies. Squeeze a little lemon and salt and pepper to taste.

On the other slice of bread, place your favorite cheese, and melt under broiler. Place on top of bread with veggies. Yum!

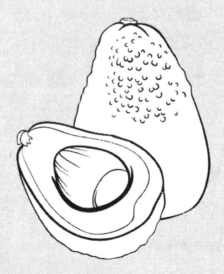

Best
Tuna Sandwich

What makes the best tuna sandwich?

#1 Quality Bread

#2 Quality Mayonnaise or Vegenaise

#3 Quality Tuna (in water)

- 2 cans **TUNA** (squeeze out water)

- ½ cup **RED ONION**, chopped

- 1/8 cup (or less) **SWEET PICKLE RELISH**

- 3 to 5 tablespoons **MAYONNAISE** or **VEGENAISE**

- 1 teaspoon **YELLOW MUSTARD**

- 100% **WHOLE WHEAT BREAD**

Optional:

- **APPLE**, chopped

- **TOASTED ALMONDS**, chopped

Mix first five ingredients well with fork.

Toast bread (optional), and spread tuna mixture on bread.

Add lettuce, sliced tomato and red onion to your sandwich.

BLTA Sandwich
Bacon, Lettuce, Tomato & Avocado

- 12 slices **APPLEWOOD SMOKED BACON** (no nitrates)

- 8 pieces of good hearty **WHOLE WHEAT BREAD**

- 3 to 5 tablespoons **MAYONNAISE** or **VEGENAISE**

- 2 small **AVOCADOS, sliced**

- 8 **TOMATO** slices

- 4 large leaves **ROMAINE LETTUCE**

- **SALT & PEPPER** to taste

Cook bacon until crisp.

Toast bread.

Spread mayo over both slices.

Layer lettuce on the bottom, next tomatoes, avocados, and lastly the bacon.

Salt and pepper to taste, and place remaining slice of toast on top.

You can cut this into quarters, or cut them in half. Serve with a hearty bowl of soup, or a large salad. Yum!

Chicken Salad Sandwich

- 4 to 6 cups cooked **CHICKEN**, chopped

- ½ cup **MAYONNAISE** or **VEGENAISE**

- ½ cup **PINK LADY APPLE**, chopped into tiny cubes

- 1/4 cup **CELERY**, chopped

- 1/8 cup **FRESH PARSLEY**, chopped

- ½ cup **SWEET ONION**, chopped

- 2 tablespoons **YELLOW MUSTARD**

- 8 pieces of good hearty **WHOLE WHEAT BREAD**

Mix all ingredients well.

Place on a hearty piece of whole wheat bread, grilled or cold.

You can also add lettuce and sliced tomato.

37

Decadent
Grilled Cheese Sandwich

- 2 slices of Quality 100% organic **WHOLE WHEAT** or **OAT BREAD**

- **MAYONNAISE** or **VEGENAISE**

- **CHEESE** of your choice; my favorite cheese is white cheddar.

- **TOMATO**, optional

- **BASIL**, optional

- **BUTTER**

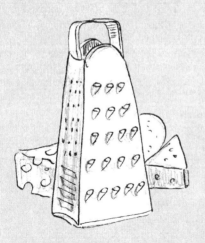

Lightly toast two slices of bread.

Spread mayonnaise on both pieces of bread.

Lay the cheese, tomato and basil... or whatever you would like, on one side of bread. Cover with the other piece of bread.

Melt some love (butter) in a pan on the lowest temperature.

Lay your sandwich into the melted butter and leave it alone until golden brown, then turn and brown the other side. You also want to make sure the cheese is melted.

Incredible
Egg Salad Sandwich

- 8 large **HARD BOILED EGGS**, chopped

- 3 stalks **CELERY**, finely chopped

- 1/4 cup **MAYONNAISE** or **VEGENAISE**

- 1 whole **SWEET ONION**, chopped

- 2 teaspoons **YELLOW MUSTARD**

- **SALT & PEPPER** to taste

- Hearty **WHOLE WHEAT BREAD**

Mix all ingredients well.

Heap large spoonfuls onto the bread and serve, Yum!

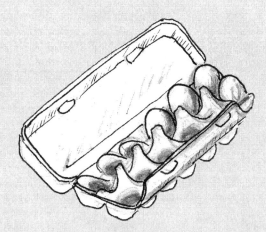

Finger Sandwiches

- **WHOLE WHEAT BREAD**

- **MAYONNAISE** or **VEGENAISE**

- **SWISS CHEESE**

- **BEEF** or **TURKEY,** sliced

Cut off bread crusts.

Spread mayonnaise on bread slices and add the cheese and meat.

Cut completed sandwich in half, and half again into finger-sized sandwiches.

French Dip Sandwiches

- Your favorite **BAGUETTE** or **FRENCH ROLL**

- 1 to 2 pounds nitrate-free, sliced **ROAST BEEF**

- **MAYONNAISE** or **VEGENAISE**

- 2 slices **JACK CHEESE**, optional

- "**BETTER THAN BULLION**" **A JUS**

• • • • • • • • • •

Slice the bread down the middle and grill under a broiler until light brown.

Heat the meat up in a pan.

Spread mayo on both sides of bread.

On one side of bread place a nice pile of meat, and on the other side place the slices of cheese.

Place it back under the broiler and melt the cheese. You may also want to sprinkle the meat with garlic salt.

Meanwhile heat up a cup of a jus.

Slice the sandwich into several pieces so that it can be dipped into the broth. Yum!

41

Tomato Basil Baguette

- Fresh **SOURDOUGH** or **FRENCH BAGUETTE**

- Laughing Cow low-fat, **CHEESE**

- **TOMATOES**, sliced

- Fresh **BASIL**

- **BALSAMIC VINEGAR**

- **GARLIC SALT & PEPPER**

Slice baguette down the middle and lay flat.

Spread cheese generously on both sides of the bread.

Place sliced ripe tomatoes on one side of the bread and basil on the other.

Drizzle tomato slices with balsamic vinegar and sprinkle with garlic salt and pepper to taste. Yum, Yum, Yum!!

Turkey Pepperoncini Sandwich

- Organic **SOURDOUGH BREAD**, sliced
- **OLIVE OIL MAYONNAISE**
- Nitrate-free **SMOKED TURKEY**, sliced
- **MONTEREY JACK CHEESE**, sliced
- **RED ONION**, sliced
- Handful of sliced **PEPPERONCINIS**
- **TOMATO**, sliced
- **SALT & PEPPER**
- **RANCH DRESSING**

Toast bread until golden brown.

Spread mayonnaise on both slices of bread.

Place turkey on one slice of bread. On other slice, place cheese, red onions and pepperoncinis.

Place both sides of sandwich under grill until cheese is melted.

Add tomato slices, salt and pepper and ranch dressing.

Cut in half and enjoy!

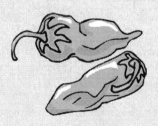

Tacos, Enchiladas & Empanadas

Black Bean & Cheese Enchiladas

- 2 tablespoons COCONUT OIL
- 1 whole SWEET ONION, chopped
- ½ bunch CILANTRO, chopped
- 2 cloves GARLIC, minced
- 1 can of organic BLACK BEANS
- 1 can of ENCHILADA SAUCE
- OLIVE OIL SPRAY
- Package of CORN TORTILLAS
- 2 cups shredded JACK and CHEDDAR CHEESE
- GOOD SALSA
- SOUR CREAM
- GUACAMOLE

Preheat oven to 400°.

Heat coconut oil in a frying pan. Add onions, cilantro, garlic, and sauté until translucent.

Add black beans, ½ of the enchilada sauce, and stir well.

Spray 13" x 9" baking dish with olive oil.

Place a corn tortilla in your hand and fill with 3 tablespoons of beans and 3 tablespoons of cheese. Roll corn tortilla up and secure with a toothpick to keep it from unrolling.

Place in baking dish. Repeat and fill remainder of dish until packed. Top enchiladas with the remainder of the cheese and enchilada sauce.

Bake at 400° for 15 minutes or until lightly browned. Serve with sour cream, guacamole, homemade salsa... guild the lily! Yum!

46

Tacos

- 10 or more **CORN TORTILLA**
- 1 to 2 tablespoons **COCONUT OIL**
- **REFRIED BLACK BEANS**
- **CHEDDAR CHEESE**, shredded
- **LETTUCE, TOMATOES, ONIONS**, chopped
- **SPROUTS** for topping
- **GOOD SALSA**
- **LIME**

In a good fry pan, heat coconut oil.

Place one or two corn tortillas into pan and fry for a moment. Turn, add beans and cheese in the middle.

Fold one side of the taco over, and fry, then flip over and fry the other side. You can tell when they are done when the cheese starts to melt and tortillas start to brown. Remove from pan.

Fill with lettuce, tomatoes, onions, sprouts, your favorite salsa, and a spritz of lime. YUM!

47

Empanadas
Meat or Veggie Pie

Dough:

- ½ cup **COLD WATER**
- 1 **EGG**
- 1 **EGG WHITE**
- 1 teaspoon **VINEGAR**
- 3 cups **WHOLE WHEAT FLOUR** (plus a little more for kneading)
- 1 teaspoon **SALT**
- 3 tablespoons **BUTTER**

In a bowl, beat the water, egg, egg white and vinegar together. Set aside.

In a separate bowl, mix together the 3 cups of flour and salt.

Cut the butter into the flour mix with a pastry blender or two butter knives. Make a well in the center of the flour mixture and pour the egg mixture into the center. Mix with a fork until dough becomes stiff.

Turn the dough out onto a lightly floured surface. Knead it just until all the flour is incorporated and the dough is smooth.

Wrap the dough in plastic and refrigerate for at least 1 hour, but never more than 24 hours.

(This is a good time to prepare your filling—page 49.)

Prepare the work surface by lightly flouring the area where you plan to roll out the dough. Roll out dough to about the size of a small flour tortilla.

continued...

48

The fun with empanadas is that you can fill them with anything such as chili or tomatoes, basil and mozzarella cheese or left-overs like roast beef and mashed potatoes. Here is one of my favorite combinations:

Filling:

- ½ pound **GROUND BEEF**
- ½ **SWEET ONION**, chopped
- **GARLIC SALT & PEPPER** to taste
- 1 cup **MASHED POTATOES**

You can also try the following combinations:

Chicken with Swiss Cheese and Rice

———

Mozzarella Cheese, Marinara Sauce and Italian sausage

———

Onion, Shredded Beef, Peas and Mashed Potatoes.

———

Be creative and have fun!

Brown meat and onion in a large skillet, then drain fat. Add garlic salt & pepper to taste. Mix in mashed potatoes.

Spoon filling into center of rolled dough. Fold over and pinch sides closed.

Bake at 375° for 20 minutes or until brown.

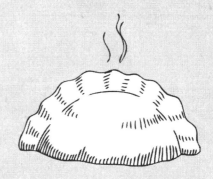

South of the Border

- 1 large, low-carb, **WHOLE GRAIN TORTILLA**
- 2 slices **MONTEREY JACK CHEESE**
- 3 slices **TOMATOES**
- **SPROUTS**
- **SALT & PEPPER**

Place tortilla on a paper plate.

Lay cheese slices on top of tortilla and microwave until cheese is melted.

Remove from microwave. Add tomatoes, sprouts and salt & pepper to taste.

You can add salsa or veggies, but this is so good you won't want to. Yum!

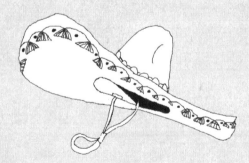

Poultry

BBQ Chicken

- 5 or more pounds of **CHICKEN**, pieces
- **SALT & PEPPER**
- Your favorite **BBQ SAUCE**

Rinse chicken and place pieces in a large soup pot. Cover with water and bring to boil on high for approximately 15 to 25 minutes, or until chicken easily fall off the bone. Remove from heat and drain.

Turn on your BBQ.

Pace boiled chicken pieces in a large bowl, cover with BBQ sauce, then place on grill.

Remember, they are already cooked, so grill them for only about 10 minutes to finish off.

Pesto Chicken

- 1 whole **CHICKEN,** or 8 to 10 pieces
- **GARLIC SALT** to taste
- **HOMEMADE PESTO** (page 82), or 1 jar quality **PESTO** (made with olive oil)

Preheat oven to 500°.

Rinse chicken. Place in baking pan (that you can cover) and sprinkle with garlic salt.

Spread pesto all over chicken.

Bake uncovered for 30 minutes, or until lightly browned.

Cover and bake for an additional 45 minutes.

Serve over brown rice or pasta.

Chicken with Coconut Milk Gravy

- 2 to 3 heaping tablespoons COCONUT OIL

- 8 to 10 pieces of CHICKEN

- 1 cup OAT FLOUR for dredging

- GARLIC SALT & PEPPER to taste

- 1 can COCONUT MILK

- 2 teaspoons BETTER THAN BULLION CHICKEN BASE, (optional)

Rinse and pat dry chicken.

Heat coconut oil in a large fry pan.

Dredge chicken in oat flour and place it in the pan. Sprinkle it with garlic salt and pepper to taste.

Brown chicken well, then turn and brown the other side. Cover and cook on medium-low heat for 10 minutes or so, until chicken is cooked on the inside.

Remove chicken from the pan and add a can of coconut milk to the juices. Stir well and allow to simmer on low for about 10 minutes.

Add garlic salt and pepper to taste, and if you want, add **Better Than Bullion Chicken Base** for flavor.

Serve chicken on mashed potatoes and pour gravy on top. Yum!

54

Chicken on a Stick

- 3 to 4 four pounds of **BONELESS CHICKEN**
- 1 bottle **YOSHIDA'S TERIYAKI SAUCE**

Rinse and pat dry chicken.

Cut into strips and place in large Zip-lock bag with teriyaki sauce. Close bag and place in refrigerator overnight.

The next day, pour off teriyaki sauce and discard. Thread marinated chicken strips onto skewers.

Heat grill on high for 10 minutes then turn to medium.

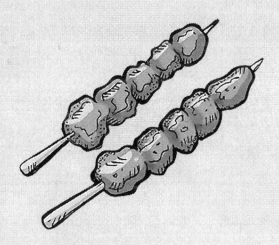

Place chicken skewers onto grill and roll over every 5 minutes until done. Yum.

Dianne's Famous
Baked Chicken

5-minute prep time!

- 1 whole (or 8 to 10 pieces) **CHICKEN**, rinsed and pat dried
- **POTATOES & CARROTS**
- 1/4 cup **BALSAMIC VINEGAR**
- 2 pkgs of natural, powdered **ITALIAN SALAD DRESSING MIX**
- **GARLIC SALT**

Preheat oven to 500°.

Place chicken in a baking pan that can be covered. Arrange potatoes and carrots around the chicken.

Pour balsamic vinegar over chicken and vegetables. Sprinkle with Italian salad dressing mix and garlic salt.

Bake uncovered for 30 minutes or until lightly browned.

Cover and bake for an additional 45 minutes or until done.

Note: Check to make sure your oven is not too hot.

Grilled Chicken & Garlic Pasta

- 8 pieces dark or light **CHICKEN** pieces, rinsed and pat dried

Marinade for grilling chicken or steak:

- ½ cup **WHITE WINE**
- ½ cup **BALSAMIC VINEGAR**
- 6 **GARLIC CLOVES**, minced
- 1/4 cup **OLIVE OIL**
- 1 tablespoon **HONEY**
- **GARLIC SALT & PEPPER** to taste

Garlic Pasta:

- 8 cups **BARRILLA PLUS PASTA** of your choice
- 10 **CHERRY TOMATOES**, chopped
- 1/4 cup fresh **BASIL**, chopped

Mix marinade and reserve half for pasta sauce.

Marinate pieces of boneless chicken 15 minutes before you grill.

Spray oil on BBQ grill. Heat grill. When good and hot, lay chicken pieces on grill.

After nicely BBQ'd, slice chicken in large pieces and serve over pasta.

Cook pasta and drain. Combine pasta, tomatoes, and basil with reserved marinade and toss.

Serve with green salad and veggies.

57

Oven Fried Chicken

- 1 1/4lb. **CHICKEN BREAST STRIPS** or 3 pounds of cut-up **CHICKEN PIECES**

- 1/4 cup **VEGENAISE** or **MAYONNAISE**

- 1 teaspoon **DRIED PARSLEY FLAKES**

- 1 tablespoon + 1/4 teaspoon **GARLIC POWDER**

- 1/4 teaspoon **PEPPER**

- 1/4 cup freshly grated **PARMESAN CHEESE**

- 1 cup **MULTIGRAIN CRACKER CRUMBS** (about 20 crackers)

Preheat oven to 400°.

Rinse chicken and pat dry. Set aside.

Stir mayonnaise, parsley, garlic powder, pepper and parsley together in a medium-size bowl.

Grind up crackers and place in a shallow bowl.

Dip chicken into the mayonnaise mixture, and then dredge into the cracker crumbs.

Place the chicken on a baking sheet. Bake the chicken strips for 20 minutes or longer for the chicken pieces. Yum!

Salsa Lime Chicken

- 1 whole **CHICKEN**, or 8 to 10 pieces
- **GARLIC SALT** to taste
- 1 clove **GARLIC**
- 1/4 cup **LIME JUICE** (bottled or fresh)
- 2 cups fresh homemade **SALSA**, or your favorite store-bought salsa

Preheat oven to 500°.

Rinse chicken. Place in baking pan (that you can cover) and sprinkle with garlic salt. Cover with chopped garlic, lime juice and salsa.

Bake uncovered for 30 minutes or until lightly browned.

Cover and bake for an additional 45 minutes.

Serve over barley, couscous, brown rice or vegetables and garnish with fresh salsa.

Teriyaki Chicken Fingers

- 6 pieces boneless, skinless **CHICKEN**
- 2 cups **TERIYAKI SAUCE**
- 1 cup **WHOLE WHEAT FLOUR**
- 1/4 cup **OLIVE OIL**

Rinse chicken and pat dry. Cut into 1 to 2 inch thick strips.

In a large plastic bag, pour 2 cups of your favorite teriyaki sauce and add chicken. Leave in the refrigerator to marinate overnight.

The next day, remove chicken from marinade. Roll chicken in flour until it is covered.

In a frying pan over medium-high heat, heat olive oil. Place floured chicken in pan and fry until golden brown. Drain pieces on a paper towel.

Eat hot or cold!

Seafood

Broiled Salmon

- 1 large SALMON FILLET
- MAYONNAISE
- GARLIC SALT & PEPPER

or...

- MELTED BUTTER
- LEMON

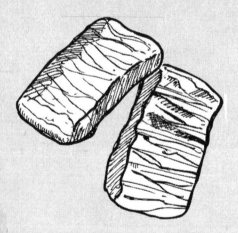

There are two simple ways to make this tasty dish:

1) Smother the fish with mayo, garlic salt and pepper. Broil or bake at 400° for about 8 minutes.

2) Cover the fish with 5 tablespoons of melted butter and sprinkle with garlic salt to taste. Squeeze lemon juice over to finish. Broil or bake just like above.

Serve with steamed asparagus and Near East Rice Pilaf—which is one thing I like to use from a box.

Fish Tacos

- 2 pounds any kind of **FISH**
- Package of **CORN TORTILLAS**, large
- **OLIVE OIL** for frying
- 2 cups **RED CABBAGE**, shredded
- 1/4 cup **CILANTRO**, coarsely chopped
- **RED SALSA**
- **TOMATOES** (optional)
- **SALT** to taste

Fry or bake the fish.

Fry tortillas in olive oil.

Place cooked fish into tortillas and top off with cabbage, cilantro, and salsa.

Add tomatoes or whatever else you want.

California Sushi Roll

- 1 cup ROSE SHORT GRAIN SUSHI RICE

- 1/4 cup SEASONED GOURMET RICE VINEGAR

- 1 AVOCADO

- 1 ENGLISH CUCUMBER

- ½ cup CRAB MEAT (real or imitation)

- MAYONNAISE to taste

- SUSHI PAPER (nori seaweed)

- LOW SODIUM SOY SAUCE

- WASABI

- PICKLED GINGER

Rinse rice under running water until water is almost clear, and then cook with 1 cup of water in a rice cooker. If you don't own a rice cooker, simmer rice in a pot, covered, for 15 to 20 minutes or until done.

You can use brown rice but it does not have the "stickiness" that is convenient for rolling the sushi—try a combination.

Place cooked rice in a bowl. Add the vinegar and mix gently while fanning the rice to cool it. Set aside.

Peel the cucumber, then slice into long, thin strips. Also peel and slice the avocado into strips. Set aside.

continued...

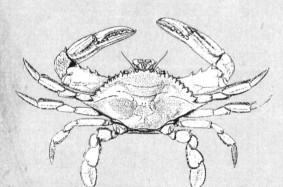

Mix crab with mayonnaise. Set aside.

Place a seaweed sheet (nori) shiny-side down on a bamboo mat. Spoon some rice on the nori sheet and spread to the edges, but leave about 1 inch at the furthest end from you.

On the end closest to you, put a line of crab mixture, cucumber and avocado across the rice.

Roll the mat beginning with the edge closest to you. Continue to roll until you reach the reserved inch you left at the furthest edge. Put some water across the reserved portion of the nori, and roll it completely over. The water will keep the nori edges together. Press down firmly on the edge to ensure a tight adhesion. Release the bamboo mat and pull it back towards you, leaving the sushi roll in place.

Dip a long, sharp knife in cold water to prevent it from sticking to the sushi rice. Slice the roll into small pieces. Make the second roll using the same method.

Serve immediately with soy sauce, wasabi and pickled ginger.

Meals on a Grill

- **FISH FILLETS** of your choice (salmon is best)
- Large pieces of **HEAVY DUTY ALUMINUM FOIL**
- **GARLIC SALT**
- **BUTTER**
- **TERIYAKI SAUCE** (optional)

Cook anything this way!

Place butter and fish in the middle of the foil, then sprinkle with garlic salt.

Form a packet rolling the sides tightly to prevent juices from leaking out.

Place the foil packet directly on the fire or grill and cook for 10 minutes.

Teriyaki sauce can also be drizzled over the salmon.

Repeat the same steps for potatoes and also veggies.

Pesto Brown Rice
with Shrimp and Mushrooms

- 2 tablespoons **BUTTER**
- 2 to 4 tablespoons **COCONUT OIL**
- 1 whole **SWEET ONION**, chopped
- 3 cloves of **GARLIC**, minced
- ½ cup **MUSHROOMS**, sliced
- 4 cups **INSTANT BROWN RICE** cooked in Chicken Broth
- 1 pound fresh **LARGE SHRIMP** with shells on
- 2 cups (more or less) **HOMEMADE PESTO** (page 84) Rinse and pat dry chicken.

In a large fry pan heat up 1 tablespoon each of butter and coconut oil.

Add onion and garlic and sauté until translucent. Add mushrooms and sauté along with garlic and onions for a few minutes.

Add rice and stir-fry for about 5 minutes. Place the stir fried rice in a bowl.

Heat pan again. Add remaining butter and coconut oil. Place all of the shrimp in the pan and cook quickly on both sides. Don't overcook the shrimp and turn only once.

Add the stir-fried rice and sauté all together for a few minutes.

Add pesto and heat for a few more minutes. Yum!

Salmon Cakes

- 4 pounds (approximately) deboned **SALMON**, baked or poached

- ½ cup good quality **MAYONNAISE** or **VEGENAISE**

- 1/8 cup **TERIYAKI SAUCE WITH GINGER**

- 2 tablespoons **DILL WEED**

- 3 **EGGS**

- 2 teaspoons **GARLIC SALT** (more or less)

- ½ cup **OAT BRAN**

- 1/8 cup **OAT FLOUR**

- 1/4 cup **OLIVE OIL**

Pull the bones from the salmon and shred into a bowl.

Add the mayonnaise, teriyaki sauce with ginger, dill weed and eggs. Mix well. Add garlic salt to taste.

Form patties, the size of a good size hamburger, patting the sides. Combine the oat bran, oat flour and garlic salt (to taste) in a bowl and dip the patties into the mixture.

Pour olive oil into a large skillet over medium heat. Add patties and brown one side. Turn only once and brown second side.

These delicious Salmon Cakes are even great cold.

Meats

Country-fried Steak
Healthy Chicken-fried Steak

- 1/4 cup **COCONUT OIL** for frying steak

- **4 CUBE STEAKS**

- ½ cup **WHOLE WHEAT FLOUR**

- **GARLIC SALT & PEPPER** to taste

Heat oil in frying pan.

Dredge steaks in flour. Season with garlic salt & pepper on both sides.

Place steaks in frying pan and brown each side. You can tell the steaks are done when you see the juices seeping from the top.

Giant Meatballs

This can also be meat loaf!

- 3 tablespoons **COCONUT OIL**
- 1/2 cup **SWEET ONION**, chopped
- 4 tablespoons **GARLIC**, chopped
- 1/2 cup fresh **PARSLEY**, chopped
- 1/2 cup **SALSA**
- 1 cup **MONTEREY JACK CHEESE**
- 2 pieces of **BREAD**, shredded
- 2 tablespoons **BALSAMIC VINEGAR**
- 3 lbs. **GROUND BEEF**
- 2 tablespoons **BASIL**, chopped

Preheat oven to 375°

In a large bowl mix all ingredients well.

Form into 2 ½ – 3" size balls.

In a frying pan, heat coconut oil and brown meatballs on all sides!

Place browned meatballs in a baking pan and bake at 375°

for approximately 25 minutes. Remove from oven and let rest for at least 15 minutes.

Sauce

- 3 cups **CHERRY TOMATOES**, cut in half
- **BALSAMIC VINEGAR**
- **GARLIC SALT**
- **PURE MAPLE SYRUP**

Poor juices from the meatballs into a bowl.

Place tomatoes on a cookie sheet and sprinkle some balsamic vinegar and a tiny bit of garlic salt on them.

Bake the tomatoes for 15 min. Remove from oven and add to the leftover juices. Squirt a little more balsamic vinegar and add the maple syrup.

Smash tomatoes with a fork and pour over the meatballs.

Oh yum!

71

Simple
Cowboy Stew

- Butter or Coconut oil
- 4 to 5 lbs. **STEW MEAT,** cubed
- 2 lbs. **RED POTATOES,** washed and cubed
- 1 bag of small **CARROTS,** peeled and washed
- ½ **SWEET ONION,** chopped
- 2 cloves **GARLIC,** minced
- 16 oz. of prepared **SALSA** (medium heat)
- **GARLIC SALT** and **PEPPER** to taste
- 2 to 3 tablespoons **PURE MAPLE SYRUP,** or to taste

Brown the stew meat in some butter or coconut oil.

Place browned meat with all the juices in a crock-pot or stew pot and add the remaining ingredients.

Set crock-pot on high heat for 6 to 7 hours. If using a stew pot, place in oven at 325° for approximately 3 to 4 hours. The stew is done when the meat falls apart.

Serve with a big green salad and homemade corn bread. Yum!

Cheaters Chili

- 1 16-oz. can **MAPLE BAKED BEANS**

- 2 14-oz. cans **BLACK BEANS**

- 1 14-oz. can **PINTO BEANS**

- 1 14-oz. can small **RED BEANS**

- 3 lbs. lean **GROUND BEEF**

- 1 16-oz. can **CRUSHED TOMATOES**

- 3 tablespoons **MAPLE SYRUP**

- **GARLIC SALT** and **PEPPER** to taste

Place ground beef in a large skillet and fry until done.

Combine the meat with rest of ingredients in a large soup pot, and warm until steaming hot. Yum!

BBQ Country-Style Pork Ribs

- 5 or more pounds of **COUNTRY PORK RIBS**
- **SALT** and **PEPPER**
- Your favorite **BBQ SAUCE**

Place washed pork ribs in large soup pot. Cover ribs with water and bring to boil on high for approximately 15 to 25 minutes, or until they start feeling like they could easily fall apart.

Turn on your BBQ or Grill, or use a grill pan.

Place boiled ribs in a large bowl and cover with BBQ sauce.

Place on the grill.

Remember, they are already cooked, so now grill them for only about 10 minutes to finish them off.

Maple Balsamic Pork Chops

- 4 tablespoons OLIVE or COCONUT OIL
- 6 to 8 nice, lean PORK CHOPS or PORK STEAKS
- OAT FLOUR
- GARLIC SALT & PEPPER to taste
- 4 tablespoons MAPLE SYRUP
- 3 tablespoons BALSAMIC VINEGAR

In a frying pan, heat oil over medium heat.

Dredge pork chops in flour and season with garlic salt and pepper on both sides.

Carefully lay pork chops in hot oil and brown both sides. Don't overcook.

Remove from heat onto serving platter. Drizzle with maple syrup and balsamic vinegar.

Optional: Serve with garlic mashed potatoes and vegetables. Also try a little fresh apple sauce on the side.

Fried Wontons

- 3 pounds low fat **GROUND BEEF** or **TURKEY**

- 2 tablespoons **GARLIC**, minced

- ½ **SWEET ONION**, shredded

- 1/4 cup **LOW SODIUM SOY SAUCE** plus more for dipping

- 4 tablespoons good quality **TERIYAKI SAUCE**

- **WONTON WRAPPERS** (large size)

- **COCONUT OIL**

Mix meat and other ingredients well with hands.

Follow directions on wonton wrapper package for stuffing and folding.

Deep fry in coconut oil over medium-high heat until lightly browned and wontons are floating.

Drain and dip in low-sodium soy sauce.

Side Dishes

BBQ Asparagus

- 1 pound **FRESH ASPARAGUS**
- 1 tablespoon **OLIVE OIL**
- ½ teaspoon **SALT**
- 1/4 teaspoon **PEPPER**

Toss together all ingredients; making sure asparagus is well coated with salt and olive oil.

Place on the grill and allow to cook for at least 5 minutes, turning occasionally. Yum!

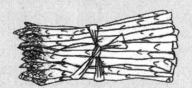

Sautéed Okra

- 2 pounds fresh **OKRA**, sliced
- 1 cup **CORN MEAL**
- 1/8 cup **OAT FLOUR**
- **GARLIC SALT** to taste
- Use **COCONUT OIL** or **OLIVE OIL** for frying.

Combine oat flour, cornmeal and garlic salt.

Dredge okra in cornmeal mixture.

In a large fry pan, heat coconut oil and place okra into the hot oil. Stir until brown.

Drain on paper towel. Yum!

BBQ Corn on the Cob

Soak the corn, husk and all, for about 15 minutes. Then gently pull back husk and remove silk (silky strands behind husk).

Brush a little **OLIVE OIL** onto the kernels then season with a little **SALT, PEPPER** and **GARLIC.**

Pull husk back over cob and place on grill. Continually turn cobs to evenly char husk on all sides.

After charred, place on warming rack or sides of grill and continue to grill with lid closed for 15 minutes. Corn is done when kernels burst when pressed. Pull back husk and enjoy!

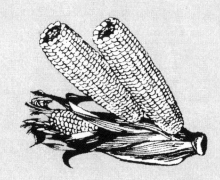

Grilled Veggies

- 2 **BELL PEPPERS** (a variety of red, orange, or green)
- 8 large **MUSHROOMS**
- 1 whole **MAUI SWEET ONION**
- 1 **ZUCCHINI**
- 1/8 cup **BALSAMIC VINEGAR**
- 1/8 cup **OLIVE OIL**
- **GARLIC SALT & PEPPER**

Slice all vegetables in 1/4 inch slices.

In a bowl, combine balsamic vinegar, olive oil, salt and pepper.

Place all veggies into bowl and coat with marinade.

Get your grill very hot, and, with a pair of tongs, place veggies onto hot grill. Sometimes it is a good idea to rub some olive oil onto grill to keep veggies from sticking. Or, use a veggie basket!

Turn only once and don't over cook. These veggies are great if they are still slightly crunchy.

Stir Fried Brown Rice

- 4 cups **BROWN RICE**, cooked
- 2 tablespoons **OLIVE OIL**
- 2 tablespoons **BUTTER**
- 1/4 pound **SNOW PEAS**
- 3 cups thinly sliced **BOK CHOY** stems and leaves
- 4 ounces fresh **SHITAKE MUSHROOMS**, stems removed and sliced
- 1 whole **SWEET ONION**
- ½ cup **GREEN ONIONS**, chopped
- 1½ tablespoons **ASIAN SESAME OIL**
- 2 tablespoons low sodium **SOY SAUCE**

Follow directions for 4 cups of brown rice. You can use quick brown rice if you don't have a rice maker.

In a wok or pan, sauté veggies in butter and olive oil.

Add cooked brown rice and sauté all together until veggies are done but still crispy.

Next add the sesame oil and soy sauce. Serve with cooked meat, chicken or fish.

Examples of veggies and meat to add: bell pepper, broccoli, green onions, mushrooms, chicken, steak, shrimp... use your imagination!

Homemade
Basil Pesto

Makes 1 cup

- 2 cups fresh **BASIL LEAVES,** packed

- ½ cup freshly grated **PARMESAN-REGGIANO** or Romano Cheese

- ½ cup **EXTRA VIRGIN OLIVE OIL** (more or less)

- 1/3 cup **PINE NUTS** or **WALNUTS**

- 3 medium sized **GARLIC CLOVES,** minced

- **SALT** and freshly ground **BLACK PEPPER** to taste

Combine basil with pine nuts and pulse a few times in a food processor, or blender. (If you are using walnuts instead of pine nuts and they are not already chopped, pulse them a few times first, before adding the basil.)

Add the garlic, pulse a few times more.

Slowly add the olive oil in a constant stream while the food processor is on. Stop to scrape down the sides of the food processor with a rubber spatula.

Add the grated cheese and pulse again until blended.

Add a pinch of salt and freshly ground black pepper to taste.

Tomato Basil Pesto

- **BASIL PESTO** (see Homemade Basil Pesto, page 84)

- 2 cups fresh **TOMATOES**, chopped

- 4 tablespoons **BALSAMIC VINEGAR**

- **SALT** and freshly ground **BLACK PEPPER** to taste

Starting with the basic pesto recipe, add the additional ingredients and blend.

This makes a delicious sauce to pour over Barilla's Plus Pasta, or chicken. And, if you add more oil and balsamic vinegar, you can turn it into a salad dressing. Yum!

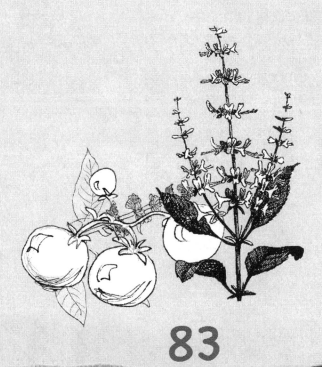

Pesto Pasta

- 1 box **BARILLA PLUS ANGEL HAIR PASTA** (multi-grain pasta)
- 1 cup **HOMEMADE BASIL PESTO** (page 82)
- **SALT** and freshly ground **BLACK PEPPER** to taste

Bring a large pot of lightly salted water to a boil. Add pasta, cook until al dente and drain.

Add pesto to pasta—the amount can vary, depending on your taste. Mix gently.

Salt and pepper to taste.

Tomato Basil Pasta

- 1 box **BARILLA PLUS ANGEL HAIR PASTA** (multi-grain pasta)

- 2 tablespoons **OLIVE OIL**

- 6 tablespoons fresh **GARLIC**, chopped

- 4 or more cups organic **CHICKEN BROTH**

- 4 cups fresh **TOMATOES**, diced and divided into two portions

- 3 cups packed **BASIL** (divided into two bunches)

- 1½ cups **PARMESAN CHEESE**, grated (save some for topping)

- **GARLIC SALT & PEPPER** to taste

Bring a large pot of lightly salted water to a boil. Add pasta, cook until al dente and drain.

In a separate pan, sauté garlic in oil over medium heat. Add chicken broth and simmer. Add half of the tomatoes, basil, and parmesan cheese, and sprinkle with garlic salt and pepper to taste. Simmer for ten minutes.

Blend in blender or use hand blender directly in the pan. You can keep this a chunky sauce, or blend it until it is smooth.

Spoon mixture over your plate of pasta and garnish with the remaining basil, tomatoes and Parmesan cheese. Serve immediately.

Best Homemade
Raw Salsa
Ever!

- 1 handful **SWEET ONION**, chopped
- 1 handful **GREEN ONIONS**, chopped
- 1 handful organic **CILANTRO**, chopped
- 1 handful raw seeded **ANAHEIM GREEN CHILE**, chopped
- 3 handfuls **RED TOMATOES**, chopped
- 2 tablespoons of fresh **GARLIC**, chopped
- 3 to 4 **LIMES**, juiced
- 1 teaspoon of **MAPLE SYRUP**
- **GARLIC SALT** to taste

Place all of the ingredients in a food processer and carefully blend with intermittent pulsing and pushing ingredients down until you get to the consistency you like.

Cranberry Relish

- 1 bag fresh **CRANBERRIES** washed and picked over

- 1 **ORANGE**

- **STEVIA** or **MAPLE SYRUP** to taste

In a food processer, place fresh cranberries, 3 tablespoons grated orange rind, the juice from ½ of an orange, and stevia or maple syrup to taste.

Pulse the food processer until desired puree. I like mine a little chunky.

This is so healthy for you. Refrigerate for up to two weeks. Use it every day or serve as a healthy desert.

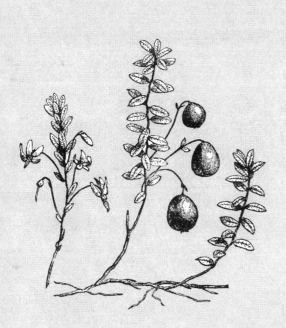

Homemade
Mashed Potatoes

- 4 pounds **RED POTATOES**
- 1 cup non-fat **SOUR CREAM**
- ½ cup real **BUTTER**
- **SALT & PEPPER**

Place potato cubes in a pot, cover with water and boil until soft, but not falling apart.

Drain potatoes, add sour cream and butter and mash well. Be careful not to over mash because red potatoes contain a lot of gluten and will become sticky.

Add salt and pepper to taste.

Coconut Cream Gravy

- **JUICES** from cooking meat
- ½ can of **COCONUT CREAM**
- **GARLIC SALT** to taste
- **PEPPER** to taste

After cooking any meat that has some left over juices in pan, add coconut cream, then season with garlic salt and pepper.

Stir over medium heat until the gravy becomes thick.

Yum!

Sweets

Brown Sugar
Shortbread

- 1 cup **SALTED BUTTER**, softened

- 1½ cups **BROWN SUGAR**, packed

- 2 cups **WHOLE WHEAT FLOUR**

- 1 teaspoon **VANILLA EXTRACT**

Preheat oven to 375°.

Using an electric mixer or mixing by hand, combine all ingredients.

On a lightly floured board, roll the dough so that it is about 1-inch thick. Cut dough with a cookie cutter, or press evenly into a shortbread pan.

If making cookies, bake for 10-15 minutes. If using a shortbread pan, bake for 30 minutes.

Hearty, Delicious
Pumpkin Cookies

- 1 cup **BUTTER**
- 2 cups **BROWN SUGAR**
- 2 **EGGS**
- 2½ cups **CANNED PUMPKIN**
- 2 teaspoons **VANILLA**
- 4 teaspoons **CINNAMON**
- 1 teaspoon **SALT**
- 2 teaspoons **BAKING SODA**
- 1 teaspoon **NUTMEG**
- 3 teaspoons **BAKING POWDER**
- 3 cups **OAT FLOUR**
- 1 cup **WHOLE WHEAT PASTRY FLOUR**
- 2 cups **CHOCOLATE CHIPS** (or more!)

Preheat oven to 350°.

Cream butter and sugar together in mixing bowl. Add eggs and beat well. Stir in pumpkin and vanilla.

In a separate bowl combine dry ingredients and whisk. Add to butter mixture, stirring to combine.

Stir in chocolate chips.

Drop spoonfuls on a greased cookie sheet and bake for 8-10 minutes.

This cookie is very cake-like and does not spread out. After the cookies cool, you can store them in an air-tight container in the refrigerator for up to two weeks. You can freeze the cookie dough for up to six months.

91

No-Bake
Missouri Cookies

- 2 cups **BROWN SUGAR**
- 3 tablespoons **COCOA**
- 1/2 cup **BUTTER**
- 1/2 cup **MILK**
- Pinch of **SALT**
- 3 cups **QUICK-COOKING OATS** (uncooked)
- 1/2 cup **CRUNCHY PEANUT BUTTER**
- 1 tablespoon **VANILLA**

Mix sugar, cocoa, butter, milk and salt in a saucepan. Cook to a rolling boil and continue cooking for one minute.

Remove from heat; whisk in peanut butter, and vanilla until well blended. Stir in oatmeal.

Drop by spoonfuls on waxed paper. Let cool until firm.

Whole Wheat
Chocolate Chip Cookies

- 21/4 cups **WHOLE WHEAT FLOUR**

- 1 teaspoon **BAKING SODA**

- 1 teaspoon **SALT**

- 1½ cups **MAPLE SUGAR** or **BROWN SUGAR**

- 1 cup **BUTTER** (2 sticks) softened

- 1 teaspoon **PURE VANILLA EXTRACT**

- 2 **EGGS**

- 2 cups **SEMI-SWEET CHOCOLATE MORSELS**

Preheat oven to 375°.

Cream butter and sugar together in mixing bowl. Add eggs and beat well. Stir in vanilla.

Whisk dry ingredients together in separate bowl and add to butter mixture, stirring to combine.

Stir in chocolate chips.

Roll into walnut-size balls and place on cookie tray lined with parchment paper.

Bake for 10 to 12 minutes until golden brown.

93

Homemade
Graham Crackers

Makes 20

- 1½ cups **WHOLE WHEAT PASTRY FLOUR**, plus more for working

- 1 cup **WHOLE WHEAT FLOUR**

- ½ cup **UNTOASTED WHEAT GERM**

- ½ teaspoon **SALT**

- 1 teaspoon **BAKING SODA**

- 1 teaspoon **GROUND CINNAMON**

- 1 cup **UNSALTED BUTTER**, softened (2 sticks)

- 3/4 cup **LIGHT BROWN SUGAR**, packed

- 2 tablespoons quality **HONEY**

Preheat oven to 350°.

Whisk flours, wheat germ, salt, baking soda, and cinnamon in a medium bowl; set aside.

With a mixer, combine butter, brown sugar and honey. Add dry ingredients and mix well.

Turn out dough onto a floured surface, and divide into quarters. Roll out each piece between 2 sheets of floured parchment paper into rectangles a bit larger than 9 by 6 inches, about 1/8 inch thick.

Using a fluted pastry wheel, trim the outermost edges of each rectangle, and divide into

continued...

three 6-by-3-inch rectangles. Pressing lightly, so as not to cut all the way through, score each piece in half lengthwise and crosswise, to form four 3-by-1 1/2-inch crackers. Stack parchment and dough on a baking sheet and chill in freezer until firm, about 20 minutes.

Remove two sheets of dough from freezer. Pierce crackers using the tines of a fork. Transfer to large baking sheets lined with parchment paper. Bake, rotating halfway through, until dark golden brown, 8 to 9 minutes. Repeat with remaining dough. Let cool on sheet 5 minutes; transfer crackers to wire racks to cool completely.

Crackers can be stored in an airtight container at room temperature up to 3 days.

Decadent Brownies

- 6 1-ounce squares **UNSWEETENED CHOCOLATE**

- 1 cup **BUTTER**, divided in half

- 1 tablespoon **PURE VANILLA**

- 3 **EGGS**

- 2½ cups **BROWN SUGAR**

- 1 cup **WHOLE WHEAT FLOUR**

- ½ tablespoon **SALT**

- 1 cup **WALNUTS**, chopped (optional)

Preheat oven to 350°.

Melt chocolate in microwave with ½ cup of the butter, add vanilla, and stir to blend. Allow to cool.

Cream remaining ½ cup butter with the eggs and sugar. Add cooled chocolate and blend well.

Fold in flour, salt, and walnuts.

Butter a 9x13 inch baking pan or spray it with olive oil, then pour mixture into pan.

Bake approximately 30 minutes.

Chocolate Truffles

Makes 30-40

BASIC TRUFFLE:

- 8 ounces of **SEMI-SWEET** or **BITTERSWEET CHOCOLATE** (quality—62% cacao or higher), well chopped into small pieces or semi-sweet Chocolate Chips

- ½ cup **HEAVY CREAM**

- 1 teaspoon **VANILLA EXTRACT**

TRUFFLE COATINGS:

- **COCOA POWDER**

- **WALNUTS**, finely chopped

- **ALMONDS**, finely chopped

In a small, heavy saucepan bring the cream to a simmer over medium heat (this may take a while, be sure to stir and scrape down the sides with a rubber spatula every few minutes).

Place the chocolate in a separate bowl. Pour the cream over the chocolate, add the vanilla, and allow to stand for a few minutes then stir until smooth. (This chocolate base is called ganache.)

Allow to cool, then place in the refrigerator for two hours.

Scoop a heaping teaspoon amount of the ganache, and quickly (as it will melt from the heat of your hands) hand-roll well-formed balls.

Place on a baking sheet lined with parchment paper and store in the refrigerator overnight.

Roll in cocoa powder and chopped nuts and serve, or place back in the refrigerator until needed.

97

Homemade Marshmallows

- 3 packages **UNFLAVORED GELATIN**
- 1 cup **ICE COLD WATER**, divided
- 12 ounces **GRANULATED SUGAR** (approximately 1½ cups)
- 1 cup **LIGHT CORN SYRUP**
- 1/4 teaspoon **SALT**
- 1 teaspoon **VANILLA EXTRACT**
- 1/4 cup **POWDERED SUGAR**
- 1/4 cup **CORNSTARCH**
- **NONSTICK COOKING SPRAY**

Place the gelatin into the bowl of a stand mixer along with ½ cup of the water. Have the whisk attachment standing by.

In a small saucepan, combine the remaining ½ cup water, granulated sugar, corn syrup and salt. Place over medium high heat, cover and allow to cook for 3 to 4 minutes.

Uncover, clip a candy thermometer onto the side of the pan and continue to cook until the mixture reaches 240°, approximately 7 to 8 minutes.

Once the mixture reaches this temperature, immediately remove from the heat.

Turn the mixer on low speed and, while running, slowly pour the sugar syrup down the side of the bowl into the gelatin mixture.

continued...

98

Once you have added all of the syrup, increase the speed to high. Continue to whip until the mixture becomes very thick and is lukewarm, approximately 12 to 15 minutes.

Add the vanilla during the last minute of whipping.

While the mixture is whipping prepare the pans as follows.

For regular marshmallows:

Combine the powdered sugar and cornstarch in a small bowl.

Lightly spray a 13 x 9-inch metal baking pan with nonstick cooking spray. Add the sugar and cornstarch mixture and move around to completely coat the bottom and sides of the pan. Return the remaining mixture to the bowl for later use.

When ready, pour the mixture into the prepared pan, using a lightly oiled spatula for spreading evenly into the pan.

Dust the top with enough of the remaining sugar and cornstarch mixture to lightly cover. Reserve the rest for later.

Allow the marshmallows to sit uncovered for at least 4 hours and up to overnight.

Turn the marshmallows out onto a cutting board and cut into 1-inch squares using a pizza wheel dusted with the confectioners' sugar mixture.

Once cut, lightly dust all sides of each marshmallow with the remaining mixture, using additional if necessary. Store in an airtight container for up to 3 weeks.

5-minute
Chocolate Strawberry Tortilla Pie

- 2 cups **CHOCOLATE CHIPS,** melted

- 6 cups **STRAWBERIES,** washed and sliced

- 3 cups **WHIPPED CREAM**

- 6 – 10" or larger **WHOLE WHEAT TORTILLAS**

Preheat oven to 300°.

Place one large tortilla on a cookie sheet and bake for ten minutes. You can also pan fry your tortilla in Olive Oil until crispy.

On a platter, cover three cooled, crisp tortillas with strawberries.

Melt chocolate in microwave and drizzle on the strawberries.

Top with whipped cream, layering it twice, and serve garnished with a whole strawberry.

This recipe is too easy!

Strawberry & Whipped Cream Parfait

- 4 cups sliced fresh organic **STRAWBERRIES**
- 3 cups homemade **WHIPPED CREAM**, sweetened with **STEVIA** or other sugar-free sweetener

Find a beautiful clear glass bowl and layer strawberries and whipped cream, all the way to the top.

If you would like, add thin slices of pound cake or angel food cake, although that will make this a high-carb recipe. The strawberries and whipped cream are delicious without the cake!

Whipped Cream

- 1 Quart **HEAVY CREAM**
- ½ teaspoon **PURE VANILLA**
- **SWEETENER**, to taste (try Stevia for sugar substitute)

Place all ingredients in a blender or the bowl of a mixer. Blend on high.

As soon as peaks form, your whipped cream is ready. If you over-whip the cream, it will turn into butter!

Chocolate Mousse

- 2 cups **WHIPPING CREAM**
- 1/4 to 1/2 cup **POWDERED COCOA**
- 1 teaspoon **PURE VANILLA EXTRACT**
- **SUGAR** or **STEVIA** to taste

In a blender or mixer, blend all ingredients on high until the mousse forms peaks. Top with Whipped Cream.

Healthy
Apple Crisp

- 6 to 8 **TART APPLES**, peeled and cubed
- 2 cups **BROWN SUGAR**
- 1 cup **OAT FLOUR**
- ½ cup **FLAX MEAL**
- 1½ cups **WHOLE WHEAT PASTRY FLOUR**
- 2 tablespoons **CINNAMON**
- 3/4 cup **SALTED BUTTER**

Preheat oven to 350°.

Place chopped apples in a 9 x 12 inch or larger baking dish that has been sprayed with olive oil.

Sprinkle 1 tablespoon of cinnamon on top of apples and some of the brown sugar.

In a large mixing bowl, combine softened butter with all dry ingredients. Use your hands and mix well; the mixture should feel crumbly. Sprinkle on top of apples and then shake a little cinnamon on top.

Bake for approximately 30 to 40 minutes. Check the apples with a fork and look for them to be soft and slightly squishy.

Top with vanilla ice cream or Whipped Cream (page 101).

103

Pineapple Sorbet

- 1 small **PINEAPPLE**, peeled and cored
- 2 tablespoons fresh **LEMON JUICE**
- 1 cup plus 2 tablespoons **SUGAR**, or **STEVIA** to taste

• • • ● ● ● • •

Cut pineapple into 2-inch pieces. Place pineapple and lemon juice in a food processor; process until smooth.

Add sugar; process 1 minute or until sugar dissolves.

Pour mixture into the freezer can of an ice-cream freezer; freeze according to manufacturer's instructions.

Spoon sorbet into a freezer-safe container. Cover and freeze 1 hour or until firm.* Garnish with mint sprigs.

*If you don't have an ice-cream freezer, use a covered metal bowl. Freeze mixture 3 hours or until it is hard on the outside but slushy in the middle. Remove it from the freezer, beat it with a whisk until smooth, and return to the freezer, covered, for 4 hours until firm.

104

Lemon Sorbet

- 1 LEMON'S PEEL, finely diced
- 1 cup WATER
- 1/2 cup SUGAR or sweeten with STEVIA to taste
- 1/2 cup LEMON JUICE
- 1/2 cup carbonated MINERAL WATER
- 6 strips of LEMON ZEST, for garnish

Unless you are using sugar, simply pour everything into a blender, and blend until the mixture becomes frothy.

If you are using sugar, add and process for 1 minute, or until sugar dissolves.

Pour into a freezer container, or plastic storage container with a lid, an put into the freezer until frozen. Yum!

Fresh Apple Sauce

- 2 of your favorite **APPLES**
- 3 shakes of **CINNAMON**
- **SWEETENER** to taste, such as Stevia, Maple Syrup, Honey, or Sugar
- 1 teaspoon of Lemon Juice

Peel apples and cut into slices.

Place apples, cinnamon, sweetener and lemon into food processor, and process until apple is the desired texture.

This sauce should be eaten soon after it is made because it can turn a little brown, and the health benefit is best when used immediately.

Beverages

Hot Spiced Apple Cider

- 6 cups **APPLE CIDER**
- ½ cup **REAL MAPLE SYRUP**
- 8 **CINNAMON STICKS**, (6 sticks for serving)
- 6 whole **ALLSPICE BERRIES**
- 1 **ORANGE PEEL**, cut into pieces
- 1 **LEMON PEEL**, cut into pieces

Pour the apple cider and maple syrup into a large stainless steel pot and heat. Cider should become very hot, but do not let it boil.

Place 2 cinnamon sticks and rest of the ingredients on a clean piece of cheese cloth and tie it closed. Add a long string onto the bundle of spices and drop into the pot of very hot cider for 30 minutes.

Take out the spice bundle and pour the cider into cute, pre-warmed mugs.

Serve with a cinnamon stick.

Healthy
Cranberry Raspberry
Sparkling Punch

- 1 quart sweetened **CRANBERRY JUICE**

- 6 **LEMONS**, juiced

- 1/4 pound **RASPBERRIES**, squashed

- 1 gallon **SODA WATER**

- 4 cups **ORANGE JUICE**, freshly squeezed

- **STEVIA**, sweeten to taste

- **ICE CUBES**

- **RASPBERRY SORBET** (optional)

Mix all ingredients and add lots of ice.

Adding some raspberry sorbet is optional—but yummy!

Lime-Strawberry Freeze

- 8 Fresh STRAWBERRIES
- 1/4 cup of fresh squeezed LEMON
- STEVIA or SUGAR to taste
- Enough ICE to make it like an Icee

Blend all ingredients in a blender until it looks like sorbet.

Add enough ice to make it the desired thickness.

Lemonade or Limeade Freeze

- 1/4 cup of fresh squeezed LEMON or LIME JUICE
- STEVIA or SUGAR to taste
- Enough ICE to make it like an Icee

In blender, blend to desired consistency. Some people like it milder and some like it very sour.

Peach Iced Tea

Make a pitcher of **BLACK TEA**. Let cool, pour over **ICE**, and add **PEACH SYRUP**. If using unsweetened peach syrup, use **STEVIA** to sweeten the tea.

Sun Tea

Fill a clear glass jar with **WATER** and **TEA BAGS**—one tea bag per cup of water. Place in a sunny spot to steep until desired color is attained (3-8 hours). Refrigerate to keep for a refreshing drink. When ready to enjoy, add items such as **FRUITS, MINT, SYRUPS,** or **SWEETENER**.

Flavored Iced Tea

Make your tea base using either **BLACK** or **GREEN TEA**. Add **FRESH FRUIT** or use your favorite **FRUIT FLAVORED SYRUP**.

Lemonade

In a pitcher of **WATER**, add desired amount of **LEMON** for desired amount of tartness. Add **SWEETENER** (such as stevia) for desired sweetness. Add **ICE**, and enjoy!

Orange Julius

- 10 oz. **ORANGE JUICE**, fresh squeezed

- 2 **ORANGES**, peeled

- 2 heaping tablespoons of **NON-FAT GREEK YOGURT**

- Sweetener, such as **MAPLE SYRUP**, or **STEVIA**

- **ICE**

In a blender, place all ingredients and puree well.

Index

*Healthy and decadent recipes
that will knock your socks off!...*

Everything That Matters in the Kitchen Cook Book
by Dianne Linderman

A cook book with simple, healthy, delicious Country Gourmet recipes in less than 20 minutes.

$19.95

A unique and beautifully crafted program...

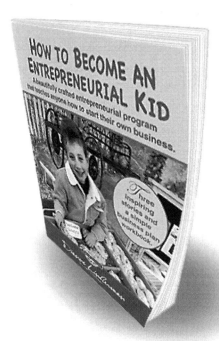

How To Become An Entrepreneurial Kid
by Dianne Linderman

A book that truly hits a nerve and fills a need by promoting financial literacy and entrepreneurial skills and attitudes for readers of many ages. This is a time when economic realities demand a kind of savvy and skill set at ever-earlier ages. "Everything in life starts with one idea!"

The series includes three enchanting, entrepreneurial storybooks and a business plan workbook for starting your own business.

$24.95

Dianne Linderman • 541-761-2007
Dianne@EverythingThatMattersRadio.com
www.EverythingThatMattersInTheKitchen.com

43248663R00070

Made in the USA
Charleston, SC
20 June 2015